The Agile Manager's Guide To

GOAL-SETTING AND ACHIEVEMENT

By Walter J. Wadsworth

Velocity Business Publishing
Bristol, Vermont USA

Velocity Business Publishing publishes authoritative works of the highest quality. It is not, however, in the business of offering professional, legal, or accounting advice. Each company has its own circumstances and needs, and state and national laws may differ with respect to issues affecting you. If you need legal or other advice pertaining to your situation, secure the services of a professional.

If you'd like additional copies of this book or a catalog of books in the Agile Manager Series™, please get in touch.

- **Write us:**
  Velocity Business Publishing, Inc.
  15 Main Street
  Bristol, VT 05443 USA

- **Call us:**
  1-888-805-8600 in North America (toll-free)
  1-802-453-6669 from all other countries

- **Fax us:**
  1-802-453-2164

- **E-mail us:**
  action@agilemanager.com

- **Visit our Web site:**
  www.agilemanager.com

The Web site contains much of interest to business people—tips and techniques, business news, links to valuable sites, and instant downloads of titles in the Agile Manager Series.

Contents

Books in the Agile Manager Series™:

Introduction

I am an utterly successful person.

Am I a millionaire? No.

Am I the CEO of a major corporation? No.

Have I done all that I want to do in life? No.

Does the president call me for advice? No.

Can I shoot a round of golf in par or better? Not even close.

So what makes me so successful?

I am succeeding in many of the areas that I've identified as important to me. These are the areas in which I set goals years— or maybe only months—ago.

For example, one of my goals early in life was to live in the country. Now I live in rural New England, which is heaven— for six months out of the year, anyway.

I always wanted to run my own business. Now I do.

I also longed for a rewarding and stable family life. I'm happily married with two lovely children. We have a lot of fun together.

Further, I never want for food and drink. I have friends to go to hockey games or concerts with. I'm near a great library with enough interesting books to keep me happy for a hundred lifetimes.

Do I pine for more? Of course. I'd love to be able to play the guitar like Eric Clapton and invest like Peter Lynch. I'd like to travel more, and do it in style. I've got some financial goals that some would consider immoderate.

But I'm making progress in these areas, and I feel rich in so many other ways that I consider goals not yet reached as minor lacks. And that's what success is all about—how you feel about your life and yourself.

Feeling successful has other benefits besides immediate happiness. For one thing, it makes you more charitable toward your neighbors and fellow human beings. For another, it encourages you to take on challenges that bring even more satisfaction. Nothing succeeds like success.

The bad news is that I don't think most people are nearly as happy and satisfied as I am.

The good news is that it's not that hard to be successful, whether in your own eyes—the most important thing—or in the eyes of others. People have been writing about how to be successful for thousands of years. They've left a rich legacy of wisdom on how to set goals and achieve them.

This book shares some of that wisdom, including the most important techniques for getting what you want.

You can read it in a few sittings, and you'll find the lessons easy to apply. If you do, and keep at it, your life will improve.

This book is for those who want more out of life—greater influence at work, more material goods, richer relationships, a deeper community life, or all of these. You can live as abundant a life as you dare envision.

In short, this book is for people who want to make their dreams come true.

Orient Yourself For Success

"Let us be of good cheer, however, remembering that the misfortunes hardest to bear are those which never come."

JAMES RUSSELL LOWELL

Chapter One

You Define Success

The Agile Manager sat in the sun on a deck chair. He had a small cooler filled with his favorite beverage next to him.

"Daddy!" said his daughter running up to him. "Look what I found in the field!" He opened his eyes and looked into his daughter's cupped hands. A tiny salamander flicked its tongue at him.

"Hey—where'd you find him?"

"He was by a big puddle—hey Janey look! Look!"

The Agile Manager's other daughter had just loped past the deck with two friends. They ran squealing toward the swing set.

"Here Daddy," said the first daughter, handing him the salamander. She ran after the others.

He put the reptile down and watch it run to the edge of the deck and disappear. Closing his eyes again, he listened to the sounds of summer—the bees collecting nectar, a blue jay squawking at an intruder, the squeak of the swings, and the children laughing.

What a life, he thought.

I have a friend I'll call Hal. Hal's father wanted him to become a lawyer. Hal loved cameras and wanted to become a photographer. His father put down his formidable foot. Hal became a lawyer.

When interviewing for his first job, the interviewer, a partner at a law firm, asked him, "Why do you want to do this?" Hal assumed it was a standard interview question—what are your motives, how committed are you, and so forth.

Hal was wrong. The partner wanted an opening to ramble on about the brutality of the legal profession and how unhappy he was.

Hal took it as an ill omen. But, with his father pushing, he soon found a job.

Hal has been a lawyer fifteen years now. The world probably sees him as successful. He makes six figures a year, drives an imported European car, and belongs to a couple of clubs. He also hates his job, where he spends sixty hours a week.

This is success?

What Do You Want?

Success is never what someone else wants for you. It's what you want.

Yet every day, people go into jobs or professions—and even hobbies and organizations—because their parents, ministers, friends, or others think it would be good for them.

The result: Lots of miserable people.

Success rarely lies in doing things for the approval of others or to become admirable in their eyes. Compliments are fleeting, and there's always the danger that you will begin to feed on the good wishes from others. When praise doesn't come on cue, you become unhappy until the next round comes along.

And there's a special place in hell (on Earth) for those who work hard for fame or riches as ends in themselves. Most celebrities tire of fan worship. They soon realize that fans project their own dreams on them and care little for the real person behind the symbol they've become. But the fans never let up.

As for those who see money as an end, hoarding and protecting it nearly killed John D. Rockefeller—until he recast his view of the purpose of money and began giving it away as fast as he made it.

Real achievement, the kind that leads to satisfaction and happiness, comes from identifying your inner dreams and desires, and working to make them come true.

The first step to becoming a successful, achieving, satisfied person is to think hard about what you really like to do, what you want out of life, and then set goals to reach your dreams.

The Agile Manager's Checklist

✔ Only you can define success.
✔ The first step toward success is to think long and hard about what you want out of life, then to set goals.
✔ Living a satisfying life is the greatest of riches.

Chapter Two

Winning Characteristics

The Agile Manager let his mind wander back to a time about five years ago.

"Come on," Ted said to the Agile Manager. "You've struck out twice now. It's time to move on to other things." Ted was a colleague from the finance department who loved to dispense "wisdom." Never mind that he'd never achieved—or stuck out his neck for—anything. "You don't want to become known as a troublemaker."

"I'm trying one more time," said the Agile Manager. "I've set up a meeting with Janet. My boss knows about it," he added. Janet was vice president in charge of product development.

"You're insane," said Ted, eyes wide. "She'll chew you up."

"I don't care. If we don't move quickly on this product, Murphy Technology will bring it out first. Look, Ted," he said leaning forward. "I want to work in a place where I can make a difference. I feel I have nothing to lose. If I get shot down, I'll—" He remembered whom he was talking to and stopped abruptly.

The Agile Manager, now back in the present, smiled as he recalled his meeting with Janet. She did chew him up—and OK'd the project.

Let's get one thing straight: Achievers in society are not usually Supermen or Wonder Women. Only a few have ever really dominated their area of focus—like Michael Jordan in basketball, Laurence Olivier in acting, Andrew Carnegie in industry, or Shakespeare in writing.

Most successful people are just like you and me. What sets them apart is that they've identified a talent and worked hard to make good use of it.

Most of us can do the same, if we want to. And wanting to makes all the difference.

Most people either fear success and what it may bring (particularly more responsibility), or they have no dreams beyond getting through the day. Pity them. But that leaves a lot of room for those who want something specific in life and are willing to work hard to get it.

The Successful Are Only a Little Bit Better

England's Roger Bannister was the first man to break four minutes in the mile back in 1954. Almost immediately, a number of people broke four minutes. He wasn't head-and-shoulders above his fellow competitors; he was only a little bit better. And he believed he could succeed.

Baseball provides a better example. We consider a .250 hitter so-so, while we glorify the .300 hitter. But what's the difference between the two? The .300 hitter gets just one extra hit in every *twenty* at bats.

That one extra hit is hard to get, obviously. Raw talent sometimes makes the difference, but often it's the work ethic of the .300 hitter. He or she employs more of the success characteristics listed in the next section.

What Defines High Achievers

Those who achieve their goals share certain characteristics. Most don't display all of the following characteristics, and many have flaws (sometimes fatal) that detract from their successes. But most display these characteristics to varying degrees.

Ponder the following list well.

Achievers Use Their Talent(s). People who succeed in extraordinary ways are those who have found the few unique talents they possess and use them to maximum benefit. Talent, alas, isn't enough. Each of us knows people with talent who let it waste away. You must combine talent with a determination to use it.

All people have at least one talent, and usually more, that sets them apart from others. It's a law of nature. If you're unhappy, especially in career, maybe you are pursuing the wrong profession or occupation.

Achievers Work Hard. Many high achievers are people with average talent who work really hard.

Working hard doesn't necessarily mean putting in long hours. It means setting goals and obtaining results, whether that takes one hour or fifty. That, in turn, means understanding what's required of the job at hand, sticking to it when others are goofing off around the water cooler or watching TV, and keeping an open and curious mind.

Best **T**ip

You have at least one talent, and probably more, that sets you apart from others.

Achievers Are Optimistic. Achievers have a can-do attitude, at least in the field they've chosen to excel in. When you're optimistic, you latch on to opportunities in a situation and use them to your advantage.

Pessimists, by contrast, blind themselves to good breaks. And they use their dour view of things as a reason to avoid acting.

Industrialist/philanthropist Andrew Carnegie often said, "All is well since all grows better." Such mottoes are a way of ensuring you expect your life to improve. If nothing else, at least tell yourself often: "I can do it."

Achievers Expect Much. As journalist/philosopher Sydney Harris once said, "Those who expect a lot out of life seem to get it."

Achievers Include Others. You can only do so much on your own. You'll achieve more, faster, if you get work done with and through others.

Achievers Remain Unflappable. Achievers take setbacks in stride. Obstacles don't deter them. They are calmer and more useful in the midst of a crisis. As Leo Tolstoy showed in *War and Peace*, the most successful and respected generals weren't tactical geniuses, but those who appeared to be calm and controlled in the midst of battle. Their demeanor inspired confidence.

Sometimes you have to give a little to get what you want. But never compromise on the big things.

Achievers Don't Compromise. The successful set their sights high and don't settle for less than they aim for.

Sometimes you have to give a little to get what you want. But don't compromise on the big things. If you want to become a doctor, for instance, don't decide that becoming a nurse is good enough. Don't settle for less than will use your talents to the utmost and make you happiest.

Achievers Focus on the Positive. Dale Carnegie said it best: "Don't criticize, condemn, or complain." For one thing, it rarely does any good. For another, when you do these things, you're highlighting your own weaknesses. Complainers tell the world they are too weak to have an impact on it.

You also get more out of people (including yourself) by appealing to their nobler aspects. Offering praise and giving credit work wonders in motivating people.

Achievers Act. Most people wait for their ship to come in, never bothering to do so much as check the schedule or buy a ticket. Others are content to dream, saying to themselves, "One day I will . . ." Achievers don't sit back and wait for things to happen in their favor. They act.

Achievers Show Determination. Winners reach way down and come up with extraordinary energy and determination when it's called for. That's the will that wins a grueling road race, the effort it takes over the course of weeks to finish an important project, or the sudden emotion necessary to finish a presentation strongly.

> **Best Tip**
>
> Change is an opportunity to exert your will and influence events. Use it to shape your life as you want it to be.

Winners rarely think afterwards. "I could've given more."

Achievers Adapt to Change. High achievers thrive on change and view it positively.

Learn to see change as an opportunity to exert your will and influence events—an opportunity to shape your life the way you want it.

Achievers Build Character. Long-term achievers practice the golden virtues that have guided the successful for all time. They are honest, gracious, charitable, and noble.

People may snicker at the virtuous. They believe you can succeed faster by ignoring values. Perhaps you can, for the short term, but operating against timeless principles catches up with you. Can a lying real-estate agent, for example, survive long in that profession? Who will give referrals?

Achievers Learn and Remain Curious. Achievers are always looking for innovative ways to employ their talents. They may do so broadly over their entire lives, or narrowly in their key area of industry. Business people, for example, know that long-term success requires innovation. Thus the good ones read voraciously, keep up to date in their technical fields, and experiment constantly.

Having a curious mind is useful. It guarantees that you won't stagnate.

Achievers Embrace Fears. Face your fears head on and overcome them. You'll profit in many ways.

I, like many, feared speaking before groups. I joined Toastmasters and overcame that fear. Having faced and conquered my worst fear strengthened and emboldened me in many ways.

Achievers Glory in Uniqueness. Achievers rarely model themselves on others. They may be inspired by others, but they know they have something unique to offer society, and society will reward them for their characteristics and talents.

Copying others rarely gets you where you want to go. David Kearns, former head of Xerox, liked to run marathons and work at a standing desk. Many mid- and just-below-senior-level executives at Xerox, he once wrote, suddenly started to run and work at standing desks. Their bootlicking got them nowhere.

Achievers Display Enthusiasm and Energy. When you love what you do, it shows. That impresses and moves others. And it propels you to great heights.

Enthusiasm can be active, like that of a Labrador retriever, or it can come in the form of quiet assurance and focus. Either way, showing enthusiasm is essential for motivating others to act in

Pick an area you love in which to excel. Your passion will generate enthusiasm and energy that moves others.

ways you want them to. You'll never persuade others of your plans or ideas, for example, by expressing them in a tired, deadpan delivery.

Achievers Take Responsibility. Blaming others for your woes is childish. High achievers take responsibility for their lives in every respect.

If you get fired or sidetracked in an organization, for example, don't blame politics or backstabbers. First look in the mirror and ask what role you played in the situation.

Achievers Persist. Anyone going after a goal faces obstacles. Achievers overcome them.

Working through obstacles results in better skills or greater strengths. And it separates you from the majority of people, who meet a few obstacles and give up.

Sometimes overcoming obstacles requires a leap of faith—or a denial of current reality. Actress Ruth Gordon makes that point in this wonderful quote: "To get it right, be born with luck or else make it. *Never* give up. Get the knack of getting people to help you and also pitch in yourself. A little money helps, but what *really* gets it right is to *never*—I repeat—*never* under any conditions face the facts."

Achievers Pursue Real Accomplishment. Some people artfully contrive to make themselves appear to be successful—by hanging out with certain people, honing their skills in self-promotion, or taking credit for the work of others. Usually they are uncovered and lose whatever influence and prestige they may have acquired.

Every achiever becomes successful through genuine accomplishment.

Achievers Practice Self-Discipline. No one ever achieved *sustained* success without self-discipline. Talent can get you to first base, but usually no farther. Achievers sacrifice to get to second base and beyond. They practice longer than others, they take classes when it's inconvenient to do so, they travel long miles to meet with a source of knowledge or hope, and they stay glued to a book when others are wasting time watching television.

Achievers Stay Organized. The successful plan to achieve. They identify a goal and work toward it systematically. Work on achieving your goals based on a daily plan.

Achievers Strive to Be the Best. Achievers in any area tend to be competitive. Some want to win at the expense of others, but most are satisfied to use competition to motivate themselves. They know it brings out their best talents—not to mention ingenuity and resourcefulness.

You Don't Need to Be a Saint

After reading the foregoing, you may be shaking your head sadly and thinking, "There's no way I can measure up to all that."

Few—maybe no one—can. But we're all capable of sustained effort over time and extraordinary effort for a short period. That means we are all capable of accomplishing our goals, no matter how grandiose.

Best Tip

Strive to be the best—but not at the expense of others.

Resourcefulness also plays an important role, as the following story illustrates, and it often takes the place of hard work. I've seen the story told only once, in Raymond C. Johnson's *The Achievers*. It may or may not be true, but I think it teaches something important.

As the story goes, at the end of World War II, Allied troops stumbled across records of all the commissioned officers in the German army. The records included the battles each officer fought in and his role in it. Each record also displayed a code—S&L, B&L, S&I, B&I. *B* stood for Brilliant, *S* for Stupid, *L* for Lazy, and *I* for Industrious.

As you might expect, the records showed that the brilliant and industrious had solid records of achievement. The stupid and lazy were poor officers, and the stupid and industrious were dangerous to themselves and others.

But the records showed that the brilliant and lazy were the most successful. For example, they devised the most innovative strategies and figured out ways to do more with fewer resources. They took the time to think about what they were doing and why.

They came up with plans for the rockets, for instance, that made life miserable for the Allied forces near the end of the war.

Think about what this story means to you. You need to commit to reaching your goals, and you need to plan how you are going to do so. But you don't have to kill yourself trying. At times, you may be more productive sitting on a beach or in a bar than plowing through work on your desk.

The Agile Manager's Checklist

✔ The successful are only a little bit better than the rest.
✔ High achievers:
  - Are optimistic;
  - Focus on the positive;
  - Act;
  - Embrace fears;
  - Take responsibility;
  - Persist.
✔ We're all capable of sustained effort over time, and extraordinary effort over the short term. You *can* succeed.

SECTION II

Set Challenging Goals

"Compromise is an essential element of politics, diplomacy, and negotiation, but not in setting and reaching goals."

NAPOLEON HILL AND MICHAEL J. RITT, JR.
IN *NAPOLEON HILL'S POSITIVE ACTION PLAN*

Chapter Three

Plan to Succeed

The Agile Manager sat at his desk at home, paying bills. He finished licking the last envelope and put the bills into a neat stack. Out of the corner of his eye he saw the list. He'd forgotten he'd taped it to the side of his filing cabinet.

It was a list of his goals. The top half of the list read:

- Learn to sail
- Become a master at giving presentations
- VP/55

He almost crossed off "learn to sail," but didn't. He'd bought an eighteen-foot day sailer and taken it out a few times, but he couldn't yet, he decided, call himself a sailor. He flipped his planner ahead to April and made a note: "Call harbor about sailing classes."

The Agile Manager volunteered to do presentations whenever asked. He knew how valuable a skill it was. Becoming a master at presentations was a lifelong goal, however, so he didn't cross that one off, either.

"VP/55" referred to his desire to be a vice president of a major corporation by age fifty-five. He frowned, not sure he was making progress there or not.

The Agile Manager had always kept a list of goals. Sometimes he looked at the list and crossed off a number of items with a disgusted look on his face. What could I have been thinking, he'd ask himself. Get down to a three handicap in golf? That would require getting out on the course every day to play or practice. Maybe when the kids are older.

But his major goals—career aspirations, investments, and hopes for his family—had stayed the same for a long, long time. And that's what success takes, he reminded himself. Sustained effort.

Most people need to identify their goals, and then create a timetable, an action plan, for reaching them.

Some—very few—succeed on talent alone and without giving a second thought to how they will go about achieving success. Such people are usually extraordinarily good at one thing—and at little else. (And none of them are reading this book, believe me!)

Somebody like chess grandmaster Bobby Fischer, for example, never needed someone or something to push him in to playing, practicing, competing, or aspiring.

The rest of us need a systematic method to achieve what we want from life. We need a plan. It's the only way to manage time effectively. This section covers creating such a plan in detail.

Write Your Own Obituary

Before you come up with a comprehensive list of goals, you need to take stock of yourself.

To get a good look at your overall ambitions in life, and what you deem important, get out a sheet of paper and a pen or sit at your computer. Detach yourself from yourself as best you can, and imagine it's fifty years hence and you've just died after an extremely successful life.

Write an obituary for yourself. Do it in the manner of a *New York Times* obituary—in depth, and with special attention to the characteristics and events that made a difference to others. Also, the job you describe should be your "dream" job.

Here's an example:

John O'Gara Hamilton passed away this morning, after a brief illness, at the age of eighty-two.

He was born in Dubuque, Iowa, in 1961. Valedictorian of his high-school class, Hamilton loved school and entered the University of Iowa in 1979 on a basketball scholarship. He graduated four years later with a degree in economics.

After moving to Boston and working for Frugality Investments in its research department for four years, he enrolled in the Harvard Business School. There he met his wife-to-be, Priscilla.

Hamilton received his MBA in 1989, married Pris, and moved to New York and worked for the Wall Street investment bank Goldman, Kinch & Company. He worked for Goldman for ten years, eventually becoming a partner.

He ended his career at Goldman, however, at age thirty-eight.

With his brother Tom and cousin Kip Schmidt, he formed a "boutique" investment bank, Hamilton, Hamilton, and Schmidt, that specialized in underwriting the public offerings of small to mid-sized natural resources companies. The firm proved so successful that by 2005 it employed eighty people.

This paper once called Hamilton "The most honest man on Wall Street" for his straight, plain talk and insistence on truth in all dealings. He was also known as an eccentric. He rode the subway to work every day, and he let others pick up the check at lunch. His colleagues never seemed to mind, however, because Hamilton was already known by that time for his charity. By the end of his life, he gave away hundreds of thousands of dollars to charities serving the poor and disadvantaged in New York. He also set up more than a dozen full scholarships, all sports-related, at the University of Iowa and other schools.

In 2014, Hamilton retired from active duty at his firm, though he stayed on as informal advisor and chairman of the board, a position he held until his death.

Before he retired, Hamilton helped his daughters succeed in the firm. One, Haley, became managing director of the firm, and another, Louisa, rose to a vice presidency.

He then devoted himself to the activities of a nonprofit organization he started, The Worldwide Wealth Foundation, to help teach entrepreneurship to citizens of "Second World" countries.

Hamilton's work at the foundation aided thousands of people. Those who went through its programs spawned no fewer than 350 companies in countries like Viet Nam, Colombia . . .

You get the picture. If you're tapping your innermost desires, your writing should flow naturally, and you shouldn't have to stop and think about what comes next. If you find yourself trying hard to make things up as you go along, stop and begin again, perhaps another day.

If you do a thorough job with your obituary, you can learn a lot about yourself. For instance, you'll see starkly what you value in life, and what your main interests are.

John Hamilton, for example, clearly appreciates education, urban life, sports, and teaching others how to create wealth. He desires a comfortable life of his own. He loves his family so much that he envisioned going into business with a brother and a cousin, and later invited his own children into the firm.

List Your Values and Goals

Analyze your obituary by making up two lists from it. Label one list "Values," and the other list "Goals."

Here are John Hamilton's lists:

VALUES

Strong family	*Good education*	*Charity*
Worthwhile work	*Public service*	*Sport*
Thrift	*Truth*	*Honesty*

GOALS

- Get an MBA
- Get a job in an investment bank on Wall Street
- Get married; have children
- Own a company
- Retire by age 55
- Set up a foundation to promote entrepreneurship
- Help children with their careers
- Work with family members

Be as comprehensive as you can. Save these lists; you'll use them later.

List Your Skills and Attributes

Are you really suited to accomplishing the goals you just outlined? Your talents need to fit your dreams. Success is all about playing to your strengths.

For example, if John Hamilton is to succeed at Harvard and on Wall Street, he should have a good head for numbers. He'll probably also need human relations (political) skills, because his line of work will require good networking and sales ability.

John also needs to inventory his character attributes. For example, he'll need to be industrious and hard-working. If he has trouble getting out of bed before 8:30 A.M., he may want to rethink his dreams. (Of course, don't forget that the lazy can at times go far.)

List your best skills and attributes. Here are John's lists:

SKILLS

- Good with numbers
- Good, logical thinking ability
- At ease with financial statements
- Know Lotus 1-2-3 and Excel
- Basic software programming ability
- Know sources for information on companies
- Know contract law
- Can manage people
- Can network and schmooze with the best of them

ATTRIBUTES

Honest	*Hardworking*	*Thrifty*
Curious	*Persistent*	*Organized*
Generous	*Serious*	*Entrepreneurial*

When you do your lists, be honest with yourself. Are your dreams realistic, given your skills and values? It's OK to decide otherwise. Remember, to succeed in life, you need to identify some real talents and employ them as profitably as you can.

Test Your Goals

Sometimes you need to test your goals and aspirations. A friend of mine wanted to get into finance; he became a stock broker. Though successful, he wasn't happy. He wanted a job that had a greater impact on the world. He went back to school to get an MBA, and now he works on Wall Street as a specialist in mergers and acquisitions.

Detours often represent money and time well spent. It's important to know what you don't want to do. It makes it easier to find your niche.

Do the Exercise Again

If you feel it might be profitable, wait a day and redo your obituary, this time following a different line of thinking. You may find that you could take any of two or three paths in life. Or five. But it's unlikely you would be equally successful in any of those five. There's probably one, or at most two, that really appeals to you. That emotional tug is telling you, "I'm the one."

But if you're like most people, you'll get it right the first time. You know what really turns you on. If so, save your obituary and various lists and proceed. After a brief interlude—a sermon on ethics—we'll see how these items are the fodder for a more comprehensive list of goals.

The Agile Manager's Checklist

✔ A rare few succeed on talent alone. The rest of us need to combine talent with hard work.

✔ Take the time to identify your goals, values, skills, and attributes. Doing an imaginary obituary helps you identify them.

✔ Test your goals out in the real world.

Chapter Four

Stand on a Foundation of Values

"We've got them now," squealed Wanda, the Agile Manager's second in command. "They'll have to lower their prices. We can cut off a good hundred bucks on each product in the line."

The Agile Manager didn't look pleased. "Wanda, we've been working with Ben and Jill for about five years. Yes, they are tough. But I've always thought they were fair. Haven't you?"

"Yes, but this is business." She gave the Agile Manager a challenging look that said, "Don't mess up a good deal that's brewing."

A temporary glut of chips on the market had potential new vendors clamoring to get the company to buy chips cheaply. Wanda wanted to use the prices they offered as a wedge to get their prime chip vendor to slash its prices.

"Let's pretend we use these new prices as a spiked board to beat them up with. They lower their prices. Then, next year, supplies tighten up again. What will they do?"

"I don't know, but they won't hold it against us if they want to keep doing business."

"Wanda, do you realize how much value Ben and Jill provide? Right now, one of their people is camped out here—in our office—

working with Anita on a redo of the 4800 series. Just last week, Ben stopped a run of another company's order midstream to expedite an order for us."

"Yeah, well it's good business." Wanda turned sullen. She knew she'd been too zealous. Somebody has to watch the bottom line around here, she told herself. But she knew he was right. "Oh OK. You're right. I'm sorry."

"I don't want you to be sorry," said the Agile Manager. "I just want everybody here to understand that taking the long view pays off." And the ethical view, he added to himself. You don't slap your friends around and expect them to remain your friends.

Before you begin setting goals for yourself, a brief word on character and ethics.

The giants on achievement and how to attain it, people like Napoleon Hill, W. Clement Stone, and Stephen Covey, are all in agreement: To succeed, you must operate in harmony with a moral code or values. You must have character.

Having character, or being principled, is essential to the long-range success that goes way beyond merely accumulating things or acquiring trophies or promotions.

True success is when someone passes you on the street and thinks, "There goes a good person." People know and remember you for your charity, helpfulness, friendship, how you've employed your talents, and what you've done for the community or society.

If they remember you for your money, it will be because your money did some good.

Yes, people can succeed by lying, cheating, and stealing. For a short while. And people can succeed by walking over others. Maybe even for a longer while. And people will show respect to anyone with a lot of money, no matter how it's gained.

Ultimately, however, whatever power or influence people without values acquire diminishes and disappears. The reason is simple: You need the good will of others to succeed. And people with poor reputations find themselves bereft of friends and contacts when they most need them the most.

The Reichmann brothers of Toronto, the power behind the now-defunct Olympia & York property-development firm, know the power of reputation. Devout Orthodox Jews, the Reichmanns long depended on a reputation for total and complete integrity in their business dealings. That integrity went a long way in helping them build a family empire worth $10 billion. (The Reichmanns eventually stumbled and fell, thanks to bad timing and, perhaps, hubris. But their reputations for honesty never fell with their bank balances.)

Be scrupulously honest in all your business dealings. Your reputation for integrity will create opportunities for you.

Think of a person you know who cuts corners—someone who lies, who has swindled another, or who in any way is untrustworthy. He doesn't walk around with a sign that says, "Swindler," but he may as well. Word gets around.

Your Character Speaks Louder than Words

Here's a fact most people don't seem to understand: Who you are and what you stand for is apparent to all at some level. We've all had intuitive flashes that said, "Don't trust this person." Or "Beware." At the very least, our feelings heightens our senses.

But when you abide by a moral code based on timeless principles, people also sense it. They feel good about doing a deal with you or getting together on a project. It just feels right to them.

Your adherence to principle, however, must be nearly flawless. There is no such thing as a "little" lie or theft. Lying on a résumé, for example, is an offense. So are habitually making personal long-distance calls at work and taking supplies home. Such things harm either people or the firm you depend on for your livelihood. Such acts brand you as dishonest, even when you think no one is around to know.

What Price Short-term Gain?

Sometimes you'll find yourself in a position of advantage. You can sell somebody something, say, for a little bit more than the item is worth. Or you can structure a deal so it's in your favor, because the other party is inexperienced or ignorant. Or maybe you and your company are so strong that it can dictate terms.

Think hard about what you're going to do. Do you want repeat customers? Do you want smart people to work for or with you again? Do you want people to treat you kindly when your luck or the economy changes?

There are no definitive guidelines in these areas. And I'm not suggesting you can't be hard-nosed and fair at the same time. My only advice: Figure out your honest bottom line—what you really need for the deal to go forward—but think long-term if you need the people you are dealing with sometime in the future.

The most successful have many people on their side pulling for them. You'll never have people pulling for you if you treat them poorly.

Common Values or Principles

What are some common values? A list follows. But if you only remember the Golden Rule—to treat others as you would have them treat you—you can bypass the list altogether. You won't need it.

BASIC VALUES TO LIVE BY

Justice	Honesty	Thrift	Empathy
Generosity	Sympathy	Fairness	Patience
Fidelity	Duty	Love	Responsibility
Charity	Helpfulness	Integrity	Trust

Some people snort in derision at the idea of living by principle—at least to themselves. But it's clear that principles are important to our lives and the health of our organizations and governments.

Stephen Covey proves this by asking whether any institution or political system, like a company or a country, could be built on the opposite of any of the basic principles.

A judiciary built on injustice? A company built on rank avarice? A friendship built on guile? A department that thrives on duplicity? No way. Any such foundation would soon cave in.

If you live according to a moral code based on timeless principles, you'll go farther—and get there faster.

The Agile Manager's Checklist

✔ To succeed in the long term, you must operate in harmony with a moral code or timeless values.

✔ True success is when someone sees you and thinks, "There goes a good person."

✔ Who you are and what you stand for is apparent to all at some level.

✔ Treat others as you would have them treat you.

Chapter Five

Set the Right Goals

The Agile Manager, feet on his desk and in a jocular mood, was questioning his desire to be vice president one day.

What does it matter? he thought, feeling smug. *I'm doing well, I've got a great family, I'm building a nice retirement fund, I have plenty to eat. What more do I need?*

Challenge! The word thundered up unexpectedly from a couple of levels beneath his conscious thinking. Yes, right. I need challenge, he thought. "Uh oh," he said aloud sitting up straight in his chair. "Am I telling myself something?"

He thought about his job heading product development for the medical instruments division of a large company.

He felt in control of it. He faced challenges daily, but they had ceased to faze him a few years ago. Problems, he knew, tended to be variations of challenges he'd met before. His biggest challenges, too, came not from pumping out good products. He had a great team of creative people who understood the market.

No, challenges tended to be organizational. Getting money and other resources, fending off ambitious fellow managers, dancing between the needs of his people and executives above him.

He liked these kinds of problems. And he liked the challenge of *influencing those around him at levels above and below.*

Yet something was missing in his life, and now he knew what it was. It was time for a change—he'd have to restructure his own job, find another one, take on additional duties.

He clapped his hands. Steve, his assistant in the outer office, startled. Then he smiled. He'd come to expect outbursts from the Agile Manager. It was his signature.

VP at fifty-five? You bet. Why not? Now, let's see. Didn't I read about an opening at headquarters? It didn't seem to fit me, but maybe I'd better take another look . . .

With the exercises in chapter three, you've done much of the trench work that needs to be done to create a set of goals. Now it's time to create a more formal and comprehensive system of goals. It's also time to begin to figure out how you're going to achieve them.

The right goals, for you, will generate enthusiasm and energy. Enthusiasm powers you toward accomplishment, and it persuades others to join you for the ride.

Best Tip

After you create a list of goals, ask of each, "Why do I want this goal?" That question keeps you honest.

Set Goals in These Areas

The exercises you did identified major goals in key areas—job, family, leisure, and so forth. But they probably didn't cover every area that's important for a rich, full life.

You should have one or two goals in each of these areas:

- Family
- Friends/social life
- Work/professional
- Community/volunteer
- Education/intellectual
- Self-improvement
- Hobby

- Leisure
- Sports
- Spiritual/Religious
- Financial

You should be able to combine categories. (Judo, for example, can combine the sport and spiritual categories. Chess combines leisure with intellectual stimulation.) If you cover the three areas that correspond roughly to the old YMCA motto—Spirit, Mind, Body—you're doing fine.

Write down the list of categories above on a piece of paper, and fit the goals you listed in chapter three into them. Create new goals for areas that have none. You should have at least one goal in each category, and not more than two or three. Any more than that makes your list too daunting. You can always add more as you achieve or remove goals.

Frame Goals Positively

Frame your goals positively, and make them specific and measurable. Not, "I want to get out of my boring old job," but, "I will have an exciting new job in the computer industry by the start of the new year." Not, "I will stop freezing in front of an audience," but, "I will become a confident and persuasive public speaker by March 1999."

Your goals should be motivating in the areas most important to you. To do that, they must challenge you. Really successful people set goals that may seem outrageous to others: "I will have $15 million by the time I'm fifty years old." Or, "I will become a producer in the movie industry within three years." Nobody who has ever amassed $15 million did so without a burning desire to succeed—and without a specific goal to do so.

Why This Goal?

When setting goals, decide what you want and when you want it. An additional question can keep you honest: Why do you want what you want?

Beware a "yes" answer to any of these: Do you want it because other people want it? Or because somebody wants you to want it? Do you want something because society confers superficial prestige upon it (money, celebrity)? Do you want something because it's a way to get revenge?

Produce a Harmonious System of Goals

The reason for setting goals in each of the categories listed above is simple: If you concentrate too heavily in any one area, it'll be hard to succeed in the one or two you really care about. Say you have a grandiose goal for your career. If you spend eighty hours a week chained to your desk, you're missing opportunities to reach your goal sooner.

For instance, by joining a charitable organization, you will probably rub shoulders with people who could steer work your way or in some way help you realize your dreams. If you committed some time to continuing education, you'd find ways to do your work more efficiently. And by making sure you build in some leisure activities, like skiing or sailing or reading mysteries, you will recharge your batteries and avoid burning out before you reach your goal.

Best Tip

Make goals measureable. Don't say, "I'll get rid of the blubber around my waist." Say, "I'll slim down fifteen pounds by July 1."

Create an Action Plan

With your goals before you, identify in specific detail how you're going to achieve them. For instance, if you're going to become a vice president of your company by the age of forty, what exactly must you do? Get an MBA? Join the right club? Get some line or overseas experience? Learn to read and understand financial statements? The more specific you are, the better. Your large goals are sometimes made up of many smaller goals, or steps.

Now it's time to get out your planner or calendar. If you don't have one, get one. Keep a list of your goals in it for easy reference.

For instance, if you have to get an MBA to become VP, set a time to request an application. Find out when the GMAT exam is and schedule it. Once you're in school, set times to study.

If you need operating experience, plot how that will become reality. Set an appointment with a person who can tell you how you can move from staff to line. Take a class in factory automation. Do what's necessary—and use your planner or calendar to make dates with destiny.

You can also use a planner to fulfill your most modest goals. For example, if one of your goals is to keep in touch with friends more by writing two letters a month, then set appointments with yourself to write those two letters.

When planning your day—writing a to-do list or making appointments in your calendar—keep your list of goals in front of you. If you don't, your grand plans will be lost among the details of the day.

Set appointments with yourself and don't let anyone or anything infringe upon them. You need quality, sustained time to reach goals.

The Agile Manager's Checklist

✔ Have goals in the major areas of your life, including work, family, leisure, spiritual.
✔ The right goals for you will generate enthusiasm and energy.
✔ Identify in specific detail how you're going to reach your goals.
✔ Create an action plan that charts when you will do the activities that lead to reaching your goals.

Chapter Six

Reach Your Goals

The Agile Manager tipped back in his chair and imagined what it would be like to be a vice president.

He saw himself getting off a company jet and into a limousine, headed to a lunch of good French food and deal making.

Whoa—is this why I want it? he wondered. *I don't think so. I'd rather eat Italian, anyway.* He "changed channels" and viewed a different scene.

Now he was seated around a conference table with an ugly, small man staring right at him. "You promised those results," barked the man. "When you make a promise around here, you keep it!"

Yuck, said the Agile Manager. *But I guess that's part of life in the executive suite.* He switched channels again.

Once again he saw himself around a conference table. Everyone was laughing at a good joke. The woman telling it continued, "So then he gets off the plane and says, 'Are we in Amshter, Amshter, Am-ster-dam yet?'" New gales of laughter.

"Thank you, Amanda," said a handsome, silver-haired man at the end of the table when the laughing died down. "All the rest of you better be just as funny when it's your turn to be meeting humorist," he said with mock menace. "Now let's get started. We have a *great new product in the AirFlow series, as you all know. The boss wants to make it fly, and he's freeing up somewhere in the vicinity of $5 million to give it a big push worldwide. So we're in the lucky position of having a bulging bank account to use as we want—as long as we get results. Who's first with ideas?"*

Ah, much better, thought the Agile Manager. That's what it's all about. Creating worthwhile products that have an impact.

Which one of these visions is real? That's easy, all of them. I just need to be aware of what I'm getting into . . .

Goals should liberate you, not shackle you.

Don't treat goals as if they were etched in stone for eternity. Be flexible; change them as necessary.

Envision Reaching Your Goals

One exercise that will help you discover whether goals are as important to you as you think they are is to visualize reaching them. Visualizing your attainment can motivate you to do what it takes to reach it—or it may help you realize you don't want to.

For example, say your goal is to move from plant manager to becoming a vice president of your 4,000-employee firm. You settle down in an easy chair, ready to envision what you'll do with your big salary and all the power you'll have. Then reality slaps you in the face.

How? Well, you begin to think about what your daily life will be like and soon you realize that being vice president means:

- Working seventy hours a week;
- Giving about ten speeches a year at just the kind of rubber-chicken dinner functions you hate;
- Traveling 200,000 miles a year and making a month-long trip to Asia each summer;
- Learning to play golf to entertain your counterparts from other companies.

And on and on. Maybe, you begin to think, that's not what I want to do with my life. "I love the smells and noises of factories," you think, "I love fixing the problems that hold up assembly lines, and I love working with blue-collar men and women. I'd lose all that if I became VP. And all that traveling would keep me from my family . . ."

Of course, visualizing success can be a great motivator. A different person may revel in the ability to play golf, travel, influence people through public speaking, and so forth.

In any case, visiting key goals in your mind often has a way of making them come true. Imagining a certain kind of future sets up certain expectations in your mind, and you work to overcome obstacles that keep you from reaching it.

Best Tip

Sit quietly and imagine what attaining a goal will feel like in all its details. Doing so is a great motivator.

There's also magic involved. Many, many people have set goals, visualized them, and then realized, upon reaching them, that doing so was uncannily just like what they imagined. Could it be that focused thinking plays a large part in how events come about?

Evaluate Your Goals

Every so often—but at least once a year—evaluate your goals. Are you making progress in each? Are some simply not important? Has some new or latent interest sparked the desire to create a new goal?

I am a runner. But for a long time I had replaced running goals with goals in cross-country skiing, golf, and bicycling. But after an interval of ten years I suddenly had the urge to run competitively again.

I replaced all my sports goals with a single one—to run a marathon. I ended up running two in one year, which satisfied my desire for competition.

One caution: Avoid being so flexible that you constantly set your sights on new goals, achieving none of them. Anyone who's achieved some goal of note has stuck to it doggedly.

What's Holding You Back?

Evaluate your progress as well as the goals themselves. If you're making no progress, why not? Are you trying hard enough? Are you working intelligently? Is the goal challenging enough? Is your method sound? Are you truly committed or do you have doubts about what you want to achieve? If you have doubts, why? Are you afraid of what success may mean?

At least once a year, evaluate your goals. Some of them may no longer "fit."

Persist

If you have particularly grand goals, they won't be achieved easily. Few become rich overnight, for instance, and those that do have most likely been working for years to become "overnight sensations."

Anybody who has achieved something significant has worked hard to overcome obstacles to success. Sometimes those obstacles include outright failures. Anecdotal evidence shows that most entrepreneurs fail once or twice before they succeed with a business.

If something is worth having, it's worth working—and persisting—for. It's as simple as that. Keep your goal in sight, and you'll find it easier to surmount the challenges that stand between you and it.

My wife wanted to bring an internationally known authority on child-rearing to our little town. She thought it was important for people to hear his message on child abuse and how they could help prevent it.

In addition, she designed the program as a fund-raiser for a day-care center for which served on the board.

Many, many, roadblocks stood in the way. The man's organization, for example, didn't seem to want to do the event. It was used to booking him for high-profile conferences and events staged by prestigious institutions. Some of his staff apparently didn't think this event would do much for his reputation.

And the event cost a small fortune—$23,000 for one day. The famous man always brought a costly entourage wherever he went, so the group could do workshops for people involved in social services.

To many, it seemed an impossibility to raise money for the event, not to mention having it pay off as a fund-raiser.

Yet my wife persisted. She wouldn't take no for an answer from the organization, and she worked tirelessly to raise money.

She began fund-raising a year ahead of the event. She had to deposit a certain amount every quarter. If she missed a payment, the event was off.

It often appeared that she would miss a date. Miraculously, she always came through, raising funds dollar by dollar from individuals in the community.

To make a long story short, she overcame any obstacle that stood in her way, and the event went off without a hitch. Two years later, people are still talking about it.

|Best *Ti*p

Once you've reached a goal, set a new one and start to achieve it.

Never Rest on Your Laurels

Many who achieve a great thing make a big mistake: They don't go after another goal.

For instance, we all know people who got a dream job, then lost it. They forgot to set new, ambitious goals that ensured they had an impact on the organization.

And we've all seen the sports star who won a gold medal or a championship—and then stagnated or slid into quagmire of alcohol or drugs.

We need goals to keep us fresh, motivated, and productive throughout our lives. Reaching a stellar goal doesn't exempt us from that rule.

It's the Journey . . .

It's been said many times and in many ways: It's the journey, not the destination.

Many achievers have reached a goal and said, "Is this it? Is this all there is to sitting in the corner office?" Or, "I thought I'd feel different behind the wheel of this car."

When you look back on your achievements, you see that the end result was like the frosting on the cake. The cake itself was made up of all the things you did to get there.

How you got there is the most interesting part of the story, anyway—the trials and obstacles you overcame, the people you had to align behind you, the ingenious maneuvers you made, the raw intelligence it took. These are the things that build character and give you wisdom, not the reward.

The Agile Manager's Checklist

✔ Regularly envision reaching your goals. Note how it will feel, from your emotions to the sights and smells around you to the people congratulating you.
✔ Evaluate your goals and change them if need be. But beware of being so flexible that you never reach any.
✔ Persist. Anything worth having is worth working for.
✔ Don't forget to have fun on the journey to success. It may be the best part.

The Fundamentals of Achievement

*"Man is always more than he can know of himself;
consequently, his accomplishments, time and again,
will come as a surprise to him."*

GOLO MANN

Chapter Seven

*T*he Power of Beliefs

The Agile Manager was working on a presentation for next month's board meeting. The thought of standing up in front of an audience made his heart race. But the adrenaline rush felt good—it was anticipation, not fear.

How different than a few years ago, he thought.

"But I can't do presentations," he'd said to his boss at the time.

"Why not?" asked his boss coldly.

"I don't know—I stand up in front of people and the words don't come out right. Then I get flustered and it gets worse. At the last one I did for the vendors, I think I made the same point three times—and not on purpose."

"I was there," said his boss. "I don't remember that. I thought you were pretty good. You show your passion for a subject—that's good. Enthusiasm counts for more than polish."

"Look, you don't have to try to make me feel better. I know I'm no good at it." The Agile Manager kept his eyes on the floor.

"I don't make idle compliments," his boss said with ice in her voice. Softening, she added, "You know, I have one tip that will help you. Instead of saying 'I can't do it,' say 'I can do it.' Tell yourself you're a good presenter. It sounds odd, but that simple

47

suggestion to yourself will open your eyes to your good points. You'll see you have something to build on."

"Really?" he said, wanting to believe her.

"Yes. I used to say to myself, 'I'm no good with numbers.' That attitude guaranteed I wouldn't be. When I got promoted into this job, people expected me to be able to talk about ratios, cash-flow projections, and stuff like that. So I'd sit down with books on how to read balance sheets and sometimes cry. To me, it was like trying to read Russian—a different language and a different alphabet.

"But I said, 'I am good with numbers! I'm going to learn this!' And I did. Now I can talk about leverage with the best of them."

How right she was, thought the Agile Manager as he popped back into the present. And how good for my career, considering I got her job, when she was promoted, based on a good speech.

Our thoughts and beliefs create the reality that we experience.

You can understand this in a basic way with a few examples. First, let's say you believe blondes are dumb.

Reality seems to back up this belief. Wherever you go, you meet dumb blondes.

In fact, your belief is organizing how you experience reality. It blinds you, for instance, from seeing the good and intelligent aspects of the blondes you meet. You don't expect to find them, so you ignore them.

Another example: Imagine you hold the belief, "I am no good at sales." That belief guarantees failure. Every rejection increases the power of that belief, and you'll find it difficult to contemplate even making a sales call.

If you can change your belief around to "I am good at sales," at least you have a fighting chance to succeed.

Beliefs also work in your favor, of course. Imagine you give a presentation. Afterwards, everyone is all smiles and people compliment you. You're not surprised because, after all, you believe "I'm quick on my feet and good in front of groups." Those beliefs brought about your success in the first place.

Chart Your Beliefs

As you can see, beliefs are powerful things for good or ill. It pays to identify them. Doing so increases your chance for success considerably.

Some of your beliefs will be easy to identify, like:

- It's good to be wealthy.
- People with a Harvard accent are smart.
- Democrats are evil.
- I'm great with numbers.

Best Tip

You can transform your life by understanding a simple concept: You create the reality you experience.

It's not that hard to chart dozens of beliefs, if you take the time, because your daily reality provides feedback on them. For example, say someone at work stabs you in the back and you find yourself saying, "Figures. People in this company would walk over their own grandmothers to get ahead." Your experience points directly to the belief you hold: People will walk on you to get ahead.

When you hold a belief like that, you're viewing reality with blinders on. You expect people to undermine you, which affects how you deal with them. They sense that attitude, and some are happy to oblige. (And you ignore those who don't, never taking it as evidence that not everybody is out to get you.)

When such feedback occurs, you believe you are viewing reality itself. But you're really viewing your beliefs about reality. If you can change your belief, you can change your reality.

Some beliefs are deeply rooted, especially those you inherited from your parents. For example, say you grew up believing that anyone who didn't go to an Ivy League school is a peon. You'll "prove" the validity of this belief over and over as you meet people from non-Ivys. In every respect, they will prove to be unfit for leadership.

Yet once you accept that yours is a belief about reality and not reality itself, you will begin to see that where one went to school has little bearing on success in life. You'll see how limiting such beliefs are and discard them.

Identify and Defuse Limiting Beliefs

It's important to identify, first, beliefs that hold you back. If you believe, for example, that you "have no head for figures," you may decide not to go after a job that has become available because it includes creating budgets and analyzing cost estimates.

To get you started with your own list, here are some sample beliefs that limit some people:

- Riches corrupt a person.
- Accountants are narrow-minded bean counters.
- Bankers are so risk-averse they need to consult a horoscope before tying their shoes.
- I'll never be smart enough to start my own business.
- I'm not good at motivating people.
- I have no talent for design.

The way to begin defusing limiting beliefs is to confront them head on. Investigating your beliefs will often take you into your past. For example, maybe you believe you aren't good with numbers because a family member or a teacher once told you that. The idea took hold.

Uncover your productive beliefs and ride them into success.

Ask yourself, "Why do I believe that?" Lay your reasons for holding that belief on the table.

Then come up with reasons why the belief is not true: "I have no problem with my own checkbook, I got all As and Bs in algebra, and for some reason it's easy for me to divide numbers in my head." Holding a spotlight on a limiting belief and coming up with reasons to refute it is often enough to banish it from your life altogether.

Some beliefs are not so easily uprooted. Gently remind yourself that any belief is a belief about reality, not reality itself. Then begin to work into your mind the belief you'd rather have. For example, "I am good with numbers." Pretend it's true even if you don't believe it. You'll start to notice when you are good with numbers, and before long your limiting belief will vanish. Incidentally, two fertile areas for exploration are your feelings about money and success. Many people have limiting beliefs in these areas for a variety of reasons.

Identify and Use Your Productive Beliefs

Now list the beliefs that can take you places. For example,

- "I've always been executive material."
- "My skill in understanding machinery is head and shoulders above most other people's."
- "I'm a great basketball player."
- "People can be trusted."

You often have productive beliefs in the areas where you are talented. Recognize such beliefs. Polish them. Remind yourself of them often.

How to Change Your Reality

By becoming more conscious of your beliefs about reality, it'll be easier to achieve your goals. You can begin to change your reality and experiences in ways that benefit you.

To do that effectively, identify beliefs you *don't* hold that could help you succeed in the ways most important to you.

Say you're known as a hard-nosed manager. You've always gotten results, but now word is that you won't go any farther in the organization. Your superiors believe you don't know how to get along with people.

First identify the beliefs that caused you to become hard-nosed in the first place. They will tumble out:

1. The people I manage are stupid.
2. Nice guys finish last.
3. The only way to get promoted in this company is and

always has been to kick butt and take no prisoners.

4. People need to be led by the nose.

5. Subordinates will take advantage of you any chance they get. You must leave them no room to maneuver.

You now know that at least one of those beliefs, number 3, isn't true. Yet for years you've believed it was bedrock reality.

Question each of these beliefs and find a few examples that refute them. You can find examples with a little digging into your memory; you just haven't focused on them.

Now imagine a different set of beliefs is the truth:

1. My people are intelligent.

2. Nice guys finish first.

3. To get ahead here, I need to get more out of my people by treating them kindly.

4. Left alone, people will do the right thing.

5. Subordinates need room to perform.

It's not easy to change beliefs you've held for years. To begin to do so, pretend that the new beliefs are true. Act in accordance with them, as painful as it may be. Be nice to people. Give them room to operate. Tell them what results you want but not how to do it. You'll begin to see that what you assumed was reality had in fact limited you.

Identifying your limiting beliefs and changing them is one of the surest ways to achieve goals that may have been elusive. It's hard work, but well worth the effort.

The Agile Manager's Checklist

✔ You create your reality through beliefs.

✔ Identify your beliefs, both productive and unproductive.

✔ Change your reality by identifying and analyzing unconstructive beliefs, and then inserting new beliefs in their places.

Chapter Eight

Overcome Setbacks

"Bill," said the Agile Manager. "I'm just wondering about that new position at headquarters. The interview was a week ago and I haven't heard from you."

There was a moment of silence at the other end. "I'm sorry, but we're giving it to Janice Preddeci." The Agile Manager's spirits fell. "I don't know if you know her—she handles new product for the outdoors group."

He sounds pretty matter-of-fact about this, thought the Agile Manager. "I don't want to put you on the spot, but was there a particular reason you didn't give it to me?"

"I'm happy to answer that. It was a good interview, as you'll recall. Neither Dan nor I could find anything wrong with you—which is about what we'd expected considering all the good things people say about you. Janice was also strong in all the right areas, plus she had experience in consumer markets. It's a different ball game than those you guys serve, and we felt that was important for this job." It sounded believable, but it was hard to know for sure.

"Well, thanks. I appreciate your candor."

"You bet. And don't worry—I'm sure something will come along for you," said Bill.

The Agile Manager hung up the phone. He was starting to feel glum so he stood up and grabbed the foam basketball and threw it to the hoop attached to the back of his door a few times.

Look on the bright side, he thought. I would have had to move. I'd have had to report to Dan, whom I don't particularly like. And I'd have to work with consumer products. He's right—that's not me.

He sat down and refined his goal—to be a VP for product development in a company selling to businesses. Better, he thought.

Some people can't understand why it's hard to reach goals. They have a goal firmly in mind and see no reason they can't move toward it boldly.

Before long, they learn that people, events, and their own ignorance stand up and block their way. Most give up, retreating to the comfort zone.

Those who achieve anything great meet challenges and surmount them. Along the way, they become wise and resilient.

Challenges Strengthen Us

A life in which there were no challenges would be boring and eventually kill off our most effective traits. (Do the idle rich contribute to society? Only rarely.)

Challenges, including setbacks and disappointments, benefit us in numerous ways. Mistakes, for instance, teach us about ourselves. Setbacks to our plans are often growth opportunities in disguise. They force us to fall back on our abilities. They stimulate creative thinking and resourcefulness.

Setbacks can also give us precise feedback on how we operate in life. A friend once told me a story about an acquaintance. Fresh out of business school, this man landed a good job with a property-leasing company and did quite well. His salary, based in part on commissions and bonuses, soon hit six figures.

His arrogance grew with his salary. He wasn't nasty, yet his attitude—that he knew it all and his success proved it—began to color his relationships. He treated support people at the company, for instance, as if they existed to serve his every whim. He didn't show the proper respect to his superiors. And when he made mistakes, he blamed others.

His insolence got him fired. It was the most bewildering moment of his life. He couldn't understand what he'd done wrong.

The situation and its lessons soon became clear. The main lesson—that success depends on the good will and support of others—burned into him deeply.

He soon found another job and is again doing well. He's also known as a nice guy and good boss.

Analyze the Setback

When you face a setback, recognize that it's a golden opportunity to learn more about yourself. But you have to take the time to analyze the situation. These questions can help you identify the cause:

- Does it have to do with my personality or how I operate?
- Is it a lack of resources (or too many)?
- Do I have the right education, skills, or experience?
- Am I connected with the right people?

Once you've identified the cause of your disappointment, remember the three Rs:

Rectify the mistake (apologize if you must)

Rethink your actions

Renew yourself by getting on with life.

One last thing: Whenever you use the word *problem,* see if you can replace it with the word *challenge* instead. Problems are dead ends that bog you down; challenges are tests of your resourcefulness. They teach you much.

Assume Things Will Work Out

People who achieve success generally assume things will eventually work out to their benefit. Their job is to figure out how to get what they want. Actually getting it is never in doubt.

By assuming things will work out, and by taking a dispassionate approach to dealing with challenges, you focus on the aspects of a situation you can affect or improve on.

Note: Assuming things will work out is different from hope. Hope sometimes helps people achieve great things, but all too often it leads to wishful thinking or prayer. I'm not against prayer, but you must ally it with action.

Rejection Isn't Personal

People often get demoralized by rejections.

A key to achieving success is to assume rejections aren't personal. A rejection, any good salesperson knows, is informative. Maybe the product or the terms on which it is sold need reworking. Maybe your approach is wrong. Maybe you're trying to get results in the wrong places.

Analyze setbacks. Be especially keen to find out whether your attitude, personality, or operating style are getting in the way of success.

Question those who reject you. You'll be surprised at how forthcoming with good advice or insights some people can be. I, for instance, was once happy to tell a job applicant why I chose someone else for the position. It was nothing personal; the other person had certain skills that won him the job.

The questioner thanked me profusely. He said he'd use the information to help him prepare for his next interview.

Don't take rejections personally. Treat them as opportunities to understand how to achieve your goals more quickly.

The Role of Luck

"Good fortune visits the prepared," goes the saying. One reason that's true: Those who have worked hard for something can spot an opportunity more easily. Sometimes it's a minor piece of the puzzle that makes completing it easier. But only someone deep into that puzzle can see the value of a single piece.

Another reason luck aids the industrious is less concrete. Every successful person can tell you that he or she got a big break, or a number of breaks, based on what appeared to be chance: A famous diva got sick and the understudy got the role and went on to bigger things. Or a financier suddenly appeared with the right amount of money at the right time.

But be aware that sometimes you're lucky when you don't get what you want. I've heard business people say that, in retrospect, it was a good thing they didn't get a certain contract—that it would have strained resources. Or it's lucky that a certain job prospect turned them down—he turned out to be a snake.

Sometimes luck takes time to show.

Get On with Life

Some people have a way of wearing their setbacks and disappointments on their sleeves. We all know people who "almost made it" in one way or another. And they tell you all about it over and over.

It's no wonder such people don't go on to better things in life; they are too busy living in the past, for one thing. For another they are just plain annoying. No one wants them around.

Never wallow in your disappointments. Analyze them, then get on with life immediately. If you lose a job, pound the pavement starting the next day. If you lose a big contract, get to work on the next sale. If you don't get a promotion, start thinking about how to get the position you want.

The Agile Manager's Checklist

✔ Expect challenges to your goals. Though seeming to be inconvenient, they help us grow.

✔ Assume that things will work out eventually. You just need to be patient.

✔ Rejection isn't personal. Accept it and get on with life.

Chapter Nine

Overcome Stress And Worry

"Good shot, Mason!" The Agile Manager lay on the floor of the squash court staring up at the ceiling. Mason had just won, 15-13.

"Another one?" asked Mason. He owned his own company and would play squash all day if the Agile Manager wanted to.

"No, some of us have to work. I've got a meeting in half an hour."

"You better hustle, then. Thursday?"

"As always. See you."

The Agile Manager ducked out of the court and heard the dull thud of the ball start up again. Mason would whack it around by himself for at least half an hour before getting back to his office.

The Agile Manager played squash Tuesdays and Thursdays. Some in the company resented seeing him leave around 10:30 in the morning and staying away for two hours. He didn't care. He came back refreshed and ready to put in a long afternoon and, sometimes, evening. He knew he was more productive both from getting a break and by staying in shape.

And he'd learned to schedule difficult meetings or phone calls on mornings before his squash game. He knew he'd relieve his *stress and get out any aggressions on the court.*

His boss had noticed. "I see that you like to pound on suppliers just before you go off to play squash. Good thinking. I used to run at noon every day, for much the same reason."

People who set goals and work hard to achieve them are prone to experiencing stress and worry. Often these result from the perceived gap between a goal and your distance from it. It may also stem from a perceived lack of control over a situation.

First let's define some terms.

Good stress: This is the stress that challenges you to do better or achieve your goal on deadline. It comes from the inside and is usually not debilitating. It is, instead, invigorating. It's the stress you feel during a sporting event, or when you're nearing the end of an important project and can feel the finish and the rewards near. You redouble your efforts and get the job done.

Bad stress: Bad stress results when you feel events are out of your control. This kind of stress often comes from the outside, or seems to. (All stress, strictly speaking, comes from inside you. That's why some people can remain calm in the face of physical danger.)

Best Tip

Don't eliminate all stress from your life—you need it to help you meet deadlines and make personal bests.

Control What You Can

Successful people have a knack for making the best of stressful situations. They do this by manipulating the elements they can grasp.

You can do the same. Say you're trying to put together a deal or project and everything is flying apart. What elements can you manipulate? How can you act? Being able to act, even in a small way, is often enough to give you a feeling of power that melts stress.

I was once caught out on Lake Michigan in a twenty-six-foot sailboat when a powerful northeaster came slamming down the lake. We—and everyone else out on the water that day—were caught by surprise; the storm wasn't due to hit until seven hours later.

We had to act fast to save ourselves and the boat. I took the

helm and pointed it into the wind while my father took down the sails. With the boat rocked by twenty-foot swells, even these simple tasks were nearly impossible.

Best Tip

Avoid perfection. That last 10 percent of effort and skill it takes to achieve it isn't worth the time.

Then we did the only thing we could. We headed for shore without the aid of the sails or the motor. (The boat was being tossed about so unmercifully that the motor rode most of the way out of the water.) The only means of acting we had at our disposal were our wits and knowledge of how the wind would push us, and the tiller.

But hanging on to the tiller and trying to anticipate our path to the shoreline were enough to give us some sense of control, saving us from feelings of hopelessness. We made it safely to harbor.

Acquiesce to the Situation

Sometimes bad situations are completely out of your hands. There is still something you can do. Give in. Totally.

Imagine you are in the CEO's office and he is berating you for your role in a failure. You desperately want to explain your reasons for doing what you did, but you know that if you open your mouth, you are finished.

What do you do? Breathe deeply and acknowledge to yourself there's absolutely nothing you can do at that moment. Acquiesce to the situation totally. Giving up all power, upon rare occasion, can you preserve you to exert it again one day.

Avoid Perfection

Another common stress-inducer is your desire to be perfect. You have a goal of perfection in your mind—like a gymnast's perfect 10—and you measure the distance between you and that 10. Inevitably, you come up short. No matter what your goal, you won't be perfect.

So don't even try. Besides, exerting yourself to get close to perfection takes much more energy than getting to 90 percent of perfection. That last 10 percent is a killer.

Stop Worrying

"Will I get what I want? Will Joan show up on time? Will I oversleep and miss the flight? What if I don't get the loan? What will the critics say? What if product X fails? What if Jerry doesn't come through for me?"

Worries can turn you old before your time. To achieve a pattern of success, you must learn to control your worrying.

Worrying does little good and can disable you. It can keep you from acting constructively when you can and should. It can cause you to give up or avoid going after a goal if you get scared of potential negative consequences.

The only good worrying can bring is if it moves you to act in ways that forward your cause.

Bil and Cher Holton, in their book *The Manager's Short Course*, offer a great method to put worry in perspective: Employ a "worry" jar.

First, get out your calendar and schedule a time to worry. 4:00 P.M. on Friday afternoon is a good time to pick.

Then, every time you worry, write out the worry on a scrap of paper and stuff it in the jar. Don't think about it again. When 4:00 on Friday comes around, get out the worry jar, pull out your worries one by one, and prepare to worry.

But you may not have to. You'll find that some of the worries had to do with things now past. Some you had blown way out of proportion. Some are laughable. Only a few, you'll find, are truly worth worrying about.

Worry about them—until 5:00 P.M. Then stop.

If you've decided that something is a real worry, then analyze it:

1. Describe your worry in detail.
2. Identify the elements of the situation.
3. Identify the elements you can do nothing about and forget about them.
4. Identify the elements you have some control over.
5. Decide what you can do with those elements.
6. Do it.

Carnegie's Time-Tested Techniques

No treatise on worry would be complete without mentioning a couple of Dale Carnegie's time-tested tricks for handling worry.

Live in day-tight compartments. An ocean liner has airtight compartments. If one compartment gets punctured, the liner can still steam safely to port.

We have our own compartments, believed Carnegie—each of the twenty-four-hour days we live in. Live in the day and that day alone, sealed up and comfortable. Do what you can that day, and leave tomorrow's worries for tomorrow.

Imagine the worst and resign yourself to it. Say you go through the worry-jar exercise and conclude you have a couple of genuine worries.

Imagine, for instance, that you own a building in which someone has a bad accident. You've heard that the person has hired the most reviled personal-injury attorney on the planet. You've tried to talk to both the injured person and the attorney, and neither will take your calls.

You even visited the attorney's office, but you were ordered to leave. You're worried sick as you wait for him to lower the boom and slap you with a huge lawsuit.

First, remember that it may not happen. He may look into the matter and decide he has no case.

But maybe he has. Maybe you were negligent. Imagine the worst: A jury finds against you and awards the plaintiff $25 million. In your mind, go through all the ramifications—you lose the building, you lose your business, and you lose your savings.

Keep going. What would you do? Well, you wouldn't lose your

> **Best Tip**
>
> Sometimes your body is telling you to be aware of a problem. Pay attention!

home or your car. You could find another job somewhere, maybe start afresh in another line of work . . .

Before you know it, you see that what you considered the end of the world really isn't. Somehow you will survive. And that thought will give you comfort.

Pay Attention to Signs of Worry—Sometimes

Your worries can be useful, especially when you begin to worry about something you don't normally worry about. Sometimes your unconscious knows something you don't and is trying to tell you to be careful.

Billionaire investor George Soros, for example, gets a pain in the back when he's made a mistake or needs to reconsider a course he's taken. His body is telling him to pay attention to something that hasn't yet reached his mind. He stops to figure out what it is.

Recreate and Get Together with Friends

I once went through an extremely unpleasant six months at a job. I did everything I could to improve the situation, without effect. In the end, I gave a lengthy notice because of a promise I had made.

Going to a job you don't want anymore can be like going to jail. I needed a daily escape.

So I ran every day at lunch time. Some days I ran three miles, some days I ran six or seven. Either way, I erased the events of the morning and made the events of the afternoon more bearable.

I shudder to think how I would have made it through those months without my running. I probably would've been sick a lot more, or even hit the bottle heavily after work.

Aerobic exercise is the best stress-buster I know. It releases endorphins, which are a hormone the body uses to deaden pain. Endorphins are behind the phenomenon called "runner's high."

You can get runner's high from biking, rollerblading, rowing, or any other exercise that gets your heart pumping and lungs expanding.

See your doctor first, then take up an exercise—even walking—that gets you moving briskly for at least thirty minutes three times a week.

Besides reducing stress, it'll reduce your waistline and expand your thinking skills.

While you're at it, ask a friend to join you. Studies show that those with a lot of good friends live longer than those without many friends. Get together with people often and laugh.

The Agile Manager's Checklist

✔ Look for levers of control in stressful situations.
✔ If there's absolutely nothing you can do—such as when your boss is chewing you out—don't resist.
✔ Avoid perfection.
✔ Worry smart: Save all worries for the end of the week, and deal with them all at once.
✔ When you worry, get busy with something else. You can't think of two things at once.

Chapter Ten

Strengthen Yourself

"Thanks, Alan. You don't know how much I appreciate this. I owe you." The Agile Manager hung up the phone and pursed his lips.

Alan, a friend at headquarters, had just let him in on the real reason he didn't get the job he'd applied for. It seems that Dan, the guy he didn't like, didn't feel much warmth for him, either. He'd also said the Agile Manager didn't have enough "style" to work at headquarters, and that he hadn't developed anyone good enough to take his place.

There was enough truth in both those statements to hurt.

The Agile Manager had always believed that achievement propelled you forward. It always had—until now. He was beginning to realize that he'd been ignoring the symbolic aspect of leading—like dressing better and saving his pointed opinions for the right time and place. That part of leading pained him.

Maybe I don't have the patience for that kind of crap, he thought. I'll have to think some more about what I want.

As for developing people to take over, only in the past two or three years had he understood this to be an important task. Before that, he'd been proud that he could "do it all." He didn't keep weak people around him, like some other managers, but he'd kept their energies focused on serving the market. No one faulted him for this; he'd done a superb job.

But I'd better step up my efforts with Wanda, he thought. People need to understand how capable she is. I bet she could take my place now and run the show beautifully. But people at headquarters don't necessarily know that.

Feeling better, he headed out to a meeting. "Hey Wanda," he said, sticking his head into her office, "Do you have time to join me for a meeting with the other department heads? It's about budgets. It'll be boring—unless two of us go after each other over a person or a line item."

Wanda's eyes brightened. "Sure!"

Back in chapter three you inventoried your skills and character attributes. Take out these lists again and study them. Are they complete?

You probably overlooked some skills. People who are naturally good at certain things often don't realize they have skills that surpass those of others.

Some people, for instance, are great storytellers without knowing it. All they know is they like to tell stories and people listen with interest or laugh a lot when they do.

But think about what skills are involved in getting a positive reaction from people through storytelling: language skills, an insightful view of what motivates people, organizational ability, and the ability to read an audience and adapt a story or joke to it.

Think hard, too, about your attributes. Our storyteller above is probably, by turns, earnest, self-confident, honest, deceptive, fun-loving, exciting—all traits that together animate the story.

Success Through Self-Knowledge

Why go through the bother of inventorying skills and attributes? Because the most successful people know themselves well. They work to develop and enhance their best attributes, and they build their careers and aspirations around particular talents.

A good friend of mine has always been a gamesman. He's played team sports all his life. He loves to play chess and other intellectual board games.

He likes to go to Atlantic City or Las Vegas and gamble. He's always in the office pool on sporting events. He's good at gambling without trying too hard—and without ever once reading a book

The most successful people know themselves well. Inventory your skills and attributes and put them to work.

on how to do better. He's got innate sense that tells him when the odds are in his favor.

He recognized early in life that he liked to play games, and that he was quite good at it. He wisely chose to avoid working for his family's manufacturing company and went instead into work at the Chicago Board of Trade. There he began trading Treasury Bill futures. All his skills came into play—the stamina he developed in sports, and the ability to remain calm in stressful situations.

Also very social, he's got an uncanny knack for charting the market's psychology. A market is, after all, a conglomeration of people's motives.

By concentrating on his best and most useful skills and abilities, he's become a major success.

Had he gone into his father's manufacturing business, would he be as successful? Probably not. And he wouldn't be nearly as happy as he is.

Success Through Self-Confidence

Self-confidence results when you use your best skills. None of us is without self-confidence in some areas. The trick practiced by many successful people is to transfer self-confidence in one area to the rest of their lives.

If you don't have self-confidence in an area, you can identify your perceived lack and fix it.

An executive recruiter I'm acquainted with tells a great story about himself. He had a terrible stutter that hindered him in all areas of his life.

A determined lad, he confronted his stutter head on. He joined a speech club and entered every contest he could. Some of his performances were incredibly painful—in a few he could hardly get more than a few words out. Yet he persisted when even the best of us would quit.

He eventually shed his stutter and won speech competitions.

In confronting his most severe lack and gaining skill, he increased his self-confidence in all areas of his life. It was a key to his ultimate success.

Act confident, even if you're not. Before long, your act will become the real thing.

Here are some time-tested ways to increase your self-confidence.

Get training. If you lack self-confidence because you lack a skill you need, go out and acquire it.

Leave mistakes behind. People often lack self-confidence because they dwell on a defeat or a big mistake they made early in life. One of the hardest, most beneficial things to do is learn to leave the past behind.

Again, some successful people have a remarkable ability to dwell in the present only, and their success is based in part on this ability.

Though not an adept in this area, I learned early on as a salesman that you'd better not carry rejections based on mistakes from one call to the next.

I remember making a call on a gift shop in a tourist area—one of nine stops that day—and doing everything wrong: calling the shopkeeper by the wrong name, not selling with her interests in mind, assuming too much about what the shop was capable of, and so forth. I didn't get the sale.

These were silly, boneheaded rookie mistakes. If I'd let them get to me, I would have had a horrible day. So I berated myself for about fifteen seconds, resolved to do better, and forgot about it. I kept my self-confidence in place.

Good thing, too, because at the third stop that day, I made the biggest sale of my life.

Act confident. Pioneer psychologist William James pointed out long ago that actions don't always have to precede feelings. In other words, you don't have to do great things to have self-confidence. You can *act* confident, and—voilà—you are. This has practical ramifications.

Say you're not at all confident about giving a speech. It's possible to convince yourself that you can give a great speech—and then do so. All it takes are constant reminders to yourself that you can not only do the job—you can do a great job.

Dress well. A maxim in climbing the career ladder is to dress the part you want, not the part you have. Want to be vice president? Shell out $1,000 for the finest pin-striped suit on the rack. And don't forget that you need different costumes for different positions or companies. A pin-striped suit may not get you far at Microsoft, for instance.

Play a role of your own choosing. Executive recruiter and author John Wareham offers a startling fact based on his experience: None of us is who we seem to be. The consummate sophisticated New Yorker, for instance, was once a farm kid in Nebraska. The white Rastafarian with dreadlocks has never been to Jamaica—he just graduated from Yale with a degree in political science. The hayseed driving a pickup truck in New Hampshire recently sold his advertising agency in Boston for $2.5 million.

How liberating! We can choose a part to play and build all kinds of self-confidence into it.

Prepare. Whenever I give a speech, I prepare. I probably put more time into speeches than most people. It's the only way I know to stand before a group bursting with self-confidence.

Shore up your confidence by doing what it takes to succeed, even if this costs you some sleep.

Success Through Good Self-Esteem

Self-confidence goes hand in hand with good self-esteem. We have to love ourselves to project confidence in all we do.

Those lacking self-esteem should:

Banish negative self-talk. If you bombard yourself with phrases like, "You'll never do it," "You're unattractive and nothing will help," or "You just don't have what it takes," you have a stiff challenge to overcome.

Overcoming negative self-talk may require professional help. Many such messages are, at root, unchallenged beliefs of others that you accepted.

Look at your beliefs and use the techniques outlined in chapter seven to change them. If you believe, for example, you are stupid, you need to start shaking the foundation out from under that belief. Once you do, the negative self-talk will begin to seem silly.

Confront yourself when you think limiting thoughts by holding an internal dialogue:

"I'll never amount to anything."

"Why do you say that?"

"Because I never have to this point."

"So that guarantees failure the rest of your life?"

"Well, maybe not. But my mother always said I wouldn't amount to much."

"And she knows everything?"

And so on. By holding a spotlight on habitual negative self-talk, you expose idiotic ideas. Isolated, they will be insupportable.

Sometimes, you have to tell yourself to shut up. "Take that talk and get out," say to yourself. "I can and will succeed."

Compliment and reward yourself. Successful people have

no problem patting themselves on the back after a job well done. "Good work, old boy. Keep it up." Or, "I knew you could do it. You've got the right skills at the right time."

And they reward themselves—with a needed vacation, a weekday afternoon round of golf, dinner out with their friends.

Banish negative thoughts about others. Sometimes when we don't feel good about ourselves, we project those feelings on others. "She's fat. I bet she never gets a date," or "What an oaf. He'll never get that promotion."

One of life's biggest wastes of time: holding grudges. Don't.

When you criticize others, you're doing so to make yourself feel better in an illegitimate way. Often, that realization is enough to improve your attitude and focus on improving yourself.

Don't hold grudges. Grudges, too, are a form of self-abuse. If you believe, for instance, that a certain person kept you from getting a promotion, you are giving that person great power over you. And you are denying your own ability to get a promotion using your own power.

Besides, as the late comic Morey Amsterdam once said, "While you're holding a grudge, they're out dancing."

Accept and enjoy compliments from others. Some people can't take a compliment. (Some, of course, take them all too well.) You say to them, "Great job!" and they say, "No, I could've done better," or, "It was Jill. She really came through." Sometimes Jill does come through, but people usually know whom to compliment.

Accept compliments and enjoy them. If you can think of nothing else, say "thank you."

Success Through Being Assertive

Successful people identify what they want and go after it. They ask for help, they knock heads (fairly) when they need to, and they take advantage of every opportunity that comes their way.

If you hesitate to state your goals or fail to act in ways that would help you reach them, you're making it harder to achieve them.

Interestingly, it's not that you're less aggressive when you're unassertive. You're simply turning it inward. The aggression remains. That's why people who let others walk over them end up abusing other people or inanimate objects.

It's okay to be aggressive. It's part of our heritage and makeup. Aggression is simply a force we can use to get what we want.

Use all the power at your command to reach your goals. Use your body and voice to make a statement about who you are and what you want. Don't forget—you can act the part you want to play and create confidence in the process.

You have the most important meeting of your life next week? Walk into it with your head held high, give a bone-crushing handshake, and speak in a loud voice.

The Agile Manager's Checklist

✔ Leave your mistakes behind. Begin each day afresh.
✔ Identify what you want and go after it. Be aggressive— and be prepared to butt heads with people along the way.
✔ Use your body and your voice to make a statement about who you are and what you want.
✔ Compliment and reward yourself for your accomplishments. You deserve it.

Achievement in Practice

"Whatever you can do, or dream you can, begin it.
Boldness has genius and magic in it. Begin it now!"

GOETHE

Chapter Eleven

Get Ahead at Work

The Agile Manager's phone buzzed. The boss.

"I heard you didn't get that job at headquarters. I'm sorry. But I'm also happy. You make me look good right where you are. Besides, I don't think that job was quite right for you. It was as much PR as anything. You wouldn't have had patience with it."

The Agile Manager steeled himself: "Thanks, but I've got to tell you: I'm ready for more. My job isn't boring, and I still love coming in every day. But I have this vague feeling—getting stronger—that I'm ready for a new challenge." *He'd never been this forthright with a boss before. He waited.*

"I hear you," *said the boss in his undisguised Texas drawl. The Agile Manager relaxed.* "I brought you up with the CEO the other day. I told him we have to take care of you or you'll jump ship. Nobody wants that to happen."

"Thanks again. But what does that mean?" *The Agile Manager wanted him to know words weren't enough.*

"I'm thinking about it. If we have to create a position, we will. Now tell me: How would Wanda do in your job? I can't quite read her."

"Wanda would be great. The troops are behind her, and . . ."

This chapter contains a number of things you need to know to get ahead on the job.

Hard Work: Not Enough

People who rise in organizations (or build businesses of their own) don't succeed on hard work alone. (Remember the stupid, industrious German officers? Disasters all.)

It's a cliché, but working smarter produces better results than merely working hard. You can do that if you:

Find out what's important. If you want to make a difference in your company, first identify its goals. If you're in a public company, these are usually financial, no matter what the company's annual report says about being "socially responsible" or "satisfying all stakeholders." Anything you can do that will increase revenues or cut costs will earn you points.

Anything else—overseeing a charitable program, for example, or instituting a democratic team system in your department—may earn you pats on the back. Those pats, however, won't propel you upward.

Even if you don't work for a public company, financial success lies in the back of the mind of every executive. And with good reason. No organization ever did a bit of good after its bankruptcy.

Find out what's important to the company or your department. Sometimes it's gross revenue, sometimes it's profitability, sometimes it's a ratio like inventory turns, sometimes it's sales of the vice president's pet product.

If that information isn't available in company documents, ask someone. It may even impress whomever you ask.

Define your contribution. As Peter Drucker always said, the most important thing an executive can do is focus on contribution. "Contribution" involves the areas in which you can influence the organization's results significantly.

Based on your understanding of what results the firm's senior executives seek, spend time thinking—alone in a quiet room on a regular basis—how you can contribute by advancing the organization's goals.

Even those low on the ladder can do something to act in harmony with senior management's wishes. All managers have any number of levers at their disposal—their budgets, the people they manage, the direction new product/service development takes, and the pursuit of quality and productivity improvements.

Is this self-evident advice? Then why do so few practice it? Everyone knows managers who work on their own pet projects when they should be doing otherwise; who are so disorganized they can't think about today, let alone tomorrow; and who can't think more broadly than the space of a 10 X 15 office. Such managers go nowhere in any sane organization.

Show that you can have an impact on the organization's overall results. It's the only way to get promoted.

Challenge the boss or company. People successful in career are not afraid to speak their minds, even when their ideas conflict with those prevalent in the company. The best bosses encourage such behavior. (The worst bosses, however, don't like to be challenged. It threatens their egos and pet ideas. At some point you may have to decide: Is it worth working for them?)

Before you spout off, do your homework. If you don't think a product will sell, be prepared to prove your point. Ditto if you don't think the company should not expand overseas.

Challenging the status quo can be dangerous. You always have to use your best human relations skills to get your ideas across in nonthreatening ways. But it's safe to say that any executive of any worthwhile company challenged widespread ideas at some point.

Get on the radar screen. Don't toil in obscurity. Even if you do effective work, make sure you get noticed. Write memos that, in passing, describe your achievements. Join important committees, volunteer for tasks no one else cares to do, write articles, or make presentations.

Most people "don't have time" to do these things. Or they are scared to do them. That's why it's sometimes easier to climb upward than you think—people drop out of the hunt, of their own choice, all the time.

Think like a boss. Most employees hand their bosses problems. The good ones either fix problems before the boss finds out, or they hand the boss a problem *and* a solution.

Also, like a boss,

- Search for better ways to do things
- Figure out ways to cut costs
- Take responsibility for results both good or bad
- Never say, "It's not my job"
- Avoid unproductive small talk
- Identify, at any moment of the work day, the most important thing you can do to advance the company's goals, and do it
- Cultivate your curious or inquisitive side—it will lead to innovations
- Work to create opportunities that benefit the company
- If the choice is between working on a problem or an opportunity, pick the opportunity every time
- Jump at the chance to assume greater responsibility.

Be entrepreneurial. Good bosses love those who come up with revenue-enhancing ideas—especially for new product lines or whole new businesses. If you think you see an opportunity, poke it in a few places to see if it yips. If initial tests—which may consist of nothing more than asking your spouse for a reaction—show the idea has promise, keep poking and prodding. Write a short business plan, test its assumptions as best you can, then make a formal proposal to your boss. If the idea is good, and you have the right skills, you may get the opportunity of a lifetime—to oversee development of your idea.

State your desires. If you've done well, maybe the powers that be are planning something for you. But don't count on it. If you want more responsibility or a particular job, ask for it.

If you're really good, you can be really bold. Al Dunlap, former CEO of Sunbeam, tells of a time he went to his boss at Kimberly-Clark and said something like, "Kimberly-Clark and I are at the crossroads." He didn't think the company was using him to his greatest capacity. It soon found him a more responsible position.

Look Ahead. Those who succeed in their careers usually spend time thinking about the industry they are in.

Do the same. Analyze what's happening and why, where things are going, which trendsetters (company and people) will become more or less influential, and how government regulations may shape business in coming years.

Manage Your Time

The preceding points in this chapter present an idealistic view of how you can get ahead at work. If you do all these things, and you work at a reasonable company, you will succeed. Guaranteed.

But something often stands between ideals and realizing them. That something is how you spend time.

The only way for you to see how much better you could do is to chart your day, minute by minute, on a piece of paper. Time logs don't lie.

Keep a piece of paper at your elbow. Every time you start or change tasks, glance at your watch and make a note. Every time you get interrupted, make a note. Leave nothing out. A typical hour might look like this:

10:00: Started filling out departmental finance report.

10:03: Sam called about charity golf tournament. Talked golf.

10:11: Back to report.

10:18: Kim walked in looking for customer survey stats.

10:22: Back to report.

10:31: Finished report, started memo on new-product effort.

10:35: Frank called from Wichita. Expedited an order that got lost.

10:48: Back to memo.

10:56: Sandy wanted to waste time talking about polo; kicked him out after three minutes.

Your time log may make you laugh or cry. You'll see why everyone talks platitudes in business yet progress runs at the speed of cold molasses.

Keep a log for a day or two—just long enough so you can see that how you think you spend your day bears no relation to reality.

To get hold of your time, you need to practice three things:

1. Keep a to-do list. Keep your short-term tasks on one side of the paper, and long-term tasks on the other.

2. Use a calendar or planner. Each morning (or at the end of the day in anticipation of the next), schedule your day based on the to-do list. Your day won't turn out exactly the way you planned, but at least you have a plan for being productive.

3. Find a quiet place where you can work uninterrupted. Hide in a spare room in the office, work at home two mornings a week, or unplug your phone. These are your most productive hours—when you can practice the ideals. *Every* successful person finds a way to secure productive hours.

> ## Best Tip
>
> Don't know where your time goes? Keep a time log. It'll astonish you—or make you cry.

Make Your Boss More Effective

You tend to rise in tandem with your boss. As she moves up, you will, too. Either you'll take her place, or she'll keep you on as a second-in-command wherever she ends up.

There's a skill in managing the boss. Your first job is to take some of the load from her shoulders.

One way to do that is to recognize her greatest strengths and take care of the things she's not good at. For example, say she's a brilliant long-range planner. But she doesn't have the computer skills to model her plans. You step in with your excellent writing and spreadsheet skills and make her ideas concrete.

You can also shoulder part of the burden by setting priorities for your work—based, of course, on her priorities.

Finally, keep her informed of anything that affects her or the department. Managers need eyes and ears beyond their own.

Work in Harmony with the 80/20 Rule

The Pareto Principle states that the majority of the effects or results come from just a few of the causes of those effects. This is what Joseph Juran calls the "vital few and trivial many," and it's a key management principle to understand. You may know this principle as the 80/20 rule. Some common examples include:

80 percent of your sales come from 20 percent of your products or customers; 80 percent of your quality problems come from 20 percent of all the things that can go wrong; 80 percent of the complaints come from 20 percent of the customers; 80 percent of the innovations come from the same 20 percent of the managers; or 80 percent of your success comes from 20 percent of your well-placed efforts.

This rule says two things:

Know the leverage points in your job and business—where a little effort produces a large result.

1. Concentrate on the products or customers that result in the biggest part of your positive results;

2. Don't try to squeeze out that last 20 percent of whatever it is you want (quality, efficiency, etc.). It'll take 80 percent of the effort.

The Pareto law is all about finding leverage points for getting work done effectively. These are different depending on your job and industry. But they exist for all.

I find, for instance, that I can get 80 percent of my work done in 20 percent of the time—if I can find uninterrupted blocks of time. Also, when I was in sales, I showered my attention on the 20 percent of the accounts that produced 80 percent of the sales.

Find Opportunities to Develop Experience

Sometimes you run up against a brick wall at work and can't advance. And for some reason it's best that you stay in your job for the time being.

Join a volunteer organization and donate your time. Much of the management and administration of such organizations is of the same type as that in a private outfit, and the "advancement" opportunities are easier. Because volunteer organizations often have to take what they can get, they are usually thrilled to have well-connected people with real business experience.

You can get great experience in such organizations, because you will have to influence events without formal authority to do so. That's great training. You'll also meet people who can aid your career, and you'll help your community at the same time.

The Agile Manager's Checklist

✔ Hard work and being "good" on the job aren't enough. You have to be smart.

✔ Know top management's organizational goals, and work in harmony with them.

✔ When in doubt about company goals, boost revenues or cut costs.

✔ Let your superiors know when you're ready for a new challenge.

✔ If you're stagnating at work, get a new job or get on the board of a nonprofit organization.

Chapter Twelve

*T*ake Prudent Risks

Wanda closed her eyes as if imagining a dire scene. *"I think it's pretty risky,"* she said.

"Of course it is," said the Agile Manager. *"But you have to keep two things in mind. First, what if we do nothing? That could be worse. Second, you can always take a risk and whittle it down to a manageable proposition."*

"I don't understand. You're proposing to take Phil and Anita, our two best developers, off their current projects and put them on an unknown. How can you reduce the risk?"

"Phil and Anita are both working on enhancements to aging products. The 'unknown,' as you call it, has customers excited. Excitement signals opportunity. Sure, we still have to fulfill on the potential we see. The biggest risk is that we can't pull it off. But what have we lost? We won't bring anything to market that doesn't fulfill the promise. So we lose some time.

"Ever read Drucker?" he continued. Wanda shook her head from side to side. *"You should. Anyway, one of his cardinal rules: Feed opportunities and starve problems."*

"But the products they are working on aren't problems," said Wanda. *"They bring in tons of money each year."*

"True, but if we keep our best people tinkering with them and

neglect opportunities, it'll catch up with us in the long term."
Wanda said nothing. But she looked pleased.

If you want to achieve any significant goal—get a promotion, launch a successful product, win a competition—you have to take some risks.

George Bernard Shaw once said, "The reasonable man adapts himself to the world; the unreasonable one persists in trying to adapt the world to himself. Therefore, all progress depends on the unreasonable man."

Risk-takers are unreasonable people. They want to show the rest of the world that something new, something innovative, is possible. Risk-takers stretch boundaries.

Don't Risk Everything

Some people think that to risk you need to "shoot from the hip," or "fly by the seat of your pants." People who do either often risk more than is necessary.

The most successful people take prudent risks. They may take a lot of risks, but none that would harm themselves irreparably. As Harvey Mackay once said, "To double your success rate, you must double your failure rate."

In the case of starting a company or introducing a product, for example, prudent risk-takers make assumptions. Then they test their assumptions every way imaginable. That reduces risk.

Good risk-takers also like to play around with and test reality. They have an idea, then use the market as a testing ground. They are very careful, however, not to bet the company on the risk.

Yet some risk always remains, and it's usually enough to scare off most people.

Not Acting: Pretty Risky

Risk-averse people face a danger, however, especially those in the for-profit business world: Doing nothing is in itself a big career risk.

Remember the parable of the talents in the Bible? A man entrusts three servants each with a certain amount of money before he goes away. One servant takes his five talents and makes five more; another servant takes two talents and makes two more; and the third buries his single talent in the backyard.

Upon his return, the man praises the first two servants. He berates the servant who buried the money.

Why? There are many valid interpretations of this wonderfully resonant story, but let's focus on one: The third servant was too cautious. He was entrusted with a resource that could have improved life, and he did nothing.

Best Tip

If you want to get ahead on the job, take a few reasonable risks each year.

Managers sit on productive resources every day, fearing to act and fail. If every manager did that, the business world would grind to a halt.

Risking money, or your talents, can be scary. But what's the alternative? No risk, no growth. For you or your company.

Risk Responsibly

Here's a seven-step method for risking responsibly:

1. Lay out the options you are considering.
2. Consider the rewards or benefits of each.
3. Identify those elements you can control or manipulate— and those you can't.
4. Ask: Can study and research improve the odds of success? (They almost always can.)
5. Ask: What if the risk fails? Can I live with the fallout?
6. Ask: What does your gut tell you? Go or no go?
7. Decide and act boldly.

Let's say you'd like to introduce a new product. Maybe it could take a number of versions—high-cost, full-featured; low-cost, no frills; or something in the middle.

What are the rewards involved with each version? Do a cost-benefit analysis. (It helps to know how to use a spreadsheet like Lotus or Excel.) One option may jump out at you. Test its profitability by estimating all costs including marketing. Does it still look good?

Don't forget—ever—that any such analysis is built on biased assumptions. You may be thrifty yourself, and thus conclude that the low-cost version makes the most sense to introduce. But if you have an upscale clientele, this may be a grave mistake. Research will help spotlight discrepancies between your biases and the market's needs.

Next, isolate all the elements of the product introduction that you can control. Most likely, you can control the design, the price, when you introduce the product, the extent and manner of distribution, the marketing campaign, and so forth.

What can't you control? People's tastes, the state of the economy, and competitor moves.

How will you reduce the risk involved in each? Study, of course. You'll watch the market closely, especially competitors and what they are up to. And you'll make a prototype of the product and conduct focus groups.

Best Tip

Use hard, numbers-based analysis *and* your intuition when you're deciding whether to go ahead with a risk.

Sometimes you can use an element of a situation you can control to neutralize an element you can't control. For instance, in this situation you can control when you introduce the new product. You'll do so when the economy and market look like they will be most accepting.

Can you contain potential problems if they occur? For instance, what if the market likes your product but rejects your price? Will you be in a position to lower it immediately or offer rebates?

At some point early in the process you must visualize in detail what will happen if you fail. Will you lose your job? Will the company go under? If so, move carefully. Sometimes you have nothing to lose by risking all. Often, however, it's foolhardy.

As you progress through the conception, prototype, and study stages, listen to your intuition. It's made up of all your business experience and knowledge, and an indescribable something else. All will combine to tell you whether you're on the right track or not.

Once you decide to act, be bold. If you start second-guessing yourself, you'll fail.

Intuition is different than wishful thinking. Wishful thinking can blind you to problems that will lead to failure.

Thus it's sometimes a blessing if you have a critic on your team who can point out all the potential pitfalls or who isn't swayed by your logic. If you don't have someone who falls into that role naturally, appoint somebody devil's advocate.

Finally, once you decide to go ahead, act boldly. If you have any misgivings, figure out why and revisit the decision. If not, you have everything to gain by rolling out your innovation with as much strength and gusto as you can muster.

It's Okay to Make Mistakes

A good boss tolerates mistakes. Not stupid mistakes, and not mistakes you've made before.

But if you do all your homework in taking on a risk, and it fails despite your best effort, there's often no career harm done. To the contrary, your failure may brand you as someone who is willing to take a chance for the good of the firm. That sets you apart from the majority.

A string of failures won't improve your career, of course, but a few can. Good bosses know that the only way the company can grow is through innovation, which is, by nature, risky. They value those who will stick their necks out upon occasion.

Keep Your Eyes Open

Well-known speaker and consultant Roger Dawson tells a great story about Conrad Hilton. Hilton, fresh out of college, went to Texas to buy a bank. He'd decided to go that route after studying his skills and the opportunities banking afforded.

He'd offered $75,000 for the bank. The owners accepted the offer, then got greedy and asked for $80,000.

Hilton wanted time to think about it. He went to a hotel across from the bank and tried to book a room.

It was full.

What's more, it sold its rooms three times a day. It seems the town was in the middle of an oil boom, and workers would come flop for eight hours and then go back to work.

Seeing a gold mine, Hilton forgot all about the bank, bought the hotel for $40,000, and started his hospitality empire.

This story has a number of worthwhile interpretations, but here's one that's key: Don't get so focused on the risk you're considering that you lose notice of what's going on around you. A better place to risk your time and energy may otherwise pass you by.

The Agile Manager's Checklist

✔ Risk-takers stretch the boundaries—both of themselves and their organizations.

✔ Make mistakes. Not stupid mistakes, but well-intentioned mistakes. Good bosses won't mind, because they know innovation requires failure.

✔ When considering a risk, make assumptions. But then test your assumptions.

✔ Don't get so focused on an opportunity that you miss a better one gliding by.

Chapter Thirteen

Stay Sharp

"There's one!" The Agile Manager pointed to the tip of a distant, towering spruce. He and his daughter Janey both raised their binoculars and focused in on the red-tailed hawk. The hawk felt their eyes and took off over the meadow. They followed its slow, lazy pattern until it alighted on a distant hickory.

"Wow," said Janey. "That's three different kinds of hawks we've seen today."

"And don't forget the snowy owl. Wait till we tell mom about that one." Both of them recalled the owl's piercing stare—and seeing it scream earthward to snatch up an unlucky mouse.

"Let's go have some lunch," said the Agile Manager.

"We have six new birds to check off on the list," said Janey. "The hawks, the owl, a ruby-throated hummingbird, and a pine system."

"That's 'siskin' muffin head," he said smiling. "And remember that we're not doing this just to check off items on a list. We want to get to know these birds—how they fly, where they nest, what they eat, the songs they sing, and all that good stuff."

"I know. Like the way those goldfinches swoop up and down and travel in packs."

"Right." They walked back to the house in silence.

Achievers don't rest on their laurels. Yesterday's star is today's has-been.

The successful work to keep their ideas and thinking processes fresh. And they work to polish their skills, knowing that knowledge and ability atrophy if not exercised.

Continue Your Education

The best way to keep your aspirations high, your thinking fresh, and your skills polished is to continue your education. There are a number of ways to do that.

Go to school. Take a class. Get a degree. Get another degree. There's a direct correlation between your formal educational attainment and your earnings. The more you learn, the more you earn.

Go to a seminar. If you're scared of numbers, for instance, go to a one-day seminar in improving your math skills or finance knowledge. One day can't hurt, and no one is going to give you a grade. Who knows—maybe you'll begin to realize you're not such a dunce after all.

Week or month-long seminars are a different thing altogether. Here you can learn something that will last. A month-long summer seminar at Wharton or Harvard on finance for nonfinancial managers, for instance, should give you really useful on-the-job tools.

These classes are demanding. You'll spend night and day immersed in the subject. And you'll have to convince your boss (or yourself) that you can afford to take the time.

And the cost! Most such programs come with a price tag that might shock Warren Buffett. But the price will also shock you into taking the class seriously and taking advantage of all it has to offer.

Offer to teach a class, write an article, or give a speech on a certain subject. You think you know a subject in depth? Teaching it to another—via class, article, or speech—will show you otherwise. Doing any of these things will force you to think hard about what you do, why you do it, what principles come into play, and when to bend the rules.

Teaching and doing are very different things, and teaching will give you a comprehensive view of your specialty that yields surprising insights. Is it any wonder that some of the world's most sought-after consultants like C. K. Prahalad or Charles Handy are academics? (Never mind that many academics couldn't help you find the bathroom with a map and flashlight. Those at the top are truly insightful.)

Read. Read trade magazines, business magazines, *The Wall Street Journal*, business books. (If all you do is read Peter Drucker, you'll be head and shoulders above everyone else. One CEO requires his senior executives to read Drucker's latest book and be able to answer questions like, "What does this mean for us? How can we put these ideas to use?")

Teach a class or write an article. You'll learn a ton—and your confidence will grow.

Some people bent on success wolf down piles of "success" and inspirational reading. Most such books are thin. If you want truly inspirational reading, try a biography of Abraham Lincoln, Winston Churchill, or anyone who faced adversity and won.

Work at Improving Your Skills

You're good at something. Can you get better at it? Of course. If you practice your skill every day on the job, though, what more can you do?

When Pat Riley was coach of the Los Angeles Lakers in the 1980s, he had to work hard to keep his team motivated. They'd won a couple of NBA championships, and they were getting complacent.

Riley kept his team honed and motivated by keeping track of some untraditional statistics. For instance, he would keep stats on such things as balls his players dove for, rebounds attempted, and so forth. He'd get the same statistics on players for other teams, and create a team competition in the process. The result? Continued excellence.

Here's a profitable game: Play around with various business ratios. Decide you're going to improve your profit margin by at least half a percent, decrease the collection period by two or three days, increase inventory turns by half a point, or improve productivity.

These kinds of games are not only fun, but they have a real impact on the business—and potentially your career.

Improve your Thinking and Writing Skills

Barry Eigen, former head of HealthCall in Wisconsin, a medical-products distributor, wrote a great book called *How to Think Like Boss*. Eigen says matter-of-factly that the people who got ahead in his company were those that could speak and write clearly and with purpose. These were the people, he says, who got the most done.

It's no wonder. Fuzzy writing and speaking reflects fuzzy thinking. When you sharpen your thinking skills, your writing and speaking improve.

But it's not clear which comes first, because learning to write well improves your thinking skills.

Take a class in writing if you think it would help, and not some one-day seminar. Take an evening course at a local college so you can devote a part of your life—like four months—to improving a skill that can really take you places.

As for speaking, try Toastmasters. It may be the greatest investment in time you ever make. You'll learn to think clearly, speak clearly, and get over any fear you have of speaking in front of groups.

Pursue a Hobby

Some very successful people have a lifelong hobby that offers a useful counterpart to their paid work. Novelist Vladimir

Nabokov, for instance, was a world-renowned collector of butterflies. My father, a successful entrepreneur, is as devoted to golf and sailing as he is to his business.

A friend who publishes a magazine also buys and sells vintage autos and automobilia. A Wall Street investment banker I know raises orchids.

Hobbies not only provide rest and relaxation. They also offer knowledge and insight that you can use in your main pursuit, or that can add to your general store of wisdom.

Any longtime sailor has been in scary situations, for example. Weathering them makes them bolder at work and more self-confident in their business dealings.

It's been said that everyone should have at least one diversion that requires observation. I read a story about a man who resolved to visit the same tree every single day and make a quick sketch of it. He improved his artistic skills, but he also saw the tree change, age, react to the seasons and weather, and combine in various ways with its environment.

Other possibilities for observing: learning to identify constellations and planets, birds, or flowers.

What good are such pursuits? They are ends in themselves. They result in a greater appreciation for life. But they will also teach you to watch people and events more closely, rather than going through the day in a cloud of your own thoughts.

The Agile Manager's Checklist

✔ Continuing your education keeps you fresh and sharp.
✔ Improve your writing and presentation skills. They, as much as anything, will propel you upward.
✔ Lose yourself in a hobby. It'll aid your career—and peace of mind—immeasurably.

Epilogue

Count Your Blessings

People with lofty goals often:

- Feel distressed at how far they are from where they want to be;
- Don't take the time to notice the beauty of the Earth and its inhabitants;
- Forget to thank those who help them along the way;
- Neglect the really important things, like family and friends.

If you're reading this book, you are probably among the most materially wealthy humans in all of history. You have much to be thankful for today. Give thanks. And know that, most likely, you will reach and surpass your goals. If you don't, perhaps you will learn more useful lessons.

Get in the daily habit of stopping what you're doing every so often to appreciate your surroundings. Marvel at the world and its secrets. No matter how much you learn and however wise you become, there is much more to learn and much more wisdom to acquire.

And don't forget: Anyone who is successful has had the help of many, many people.

Not long ago, I read an interview with one of the premier running backs in the National Football League. He told a story about one of his first years in the league. He was having a great season, and he ended up rushing for around 1,500 yards—quite a feat.

He got cocky. He started talking about how great he was and how lucky everyone on the team was to have him around.

The linemen decided to teach him a lesson. The first time he carried the ball in the next practice, the linemen didn't block the defenders. The running back got creamed way behind the line of scrimmage. To his credit, he got the message immediately. "Sorry, guys," he said in the next huddle.

And he remembered that lesson for the rest of his career.

Your success will depend on the help of others. Give your thanks freely to people who support and further your efforts. Show your appreciation by writing them notes, giving them small gifts, or by letting them in on your plans.

When you accomplish an amazing thing, like roll out a smashing new product or land a major contract, let those who helped share in the glory.

Last, let your friends and family know how much you love them. They are your real riches.